Rosemary Stones

Too Close Encounters
and what to do about them

A Magnet Book

First published as a Magnet paperback in 1987
by Methuen Children's Books Ltd
11 New Fetter Lane, London EC4P 4EE
Copyright © 1987 Rosemary Stones
Printed in Great Britain
Richard Clay Ltd, Bungay, Suffolk

British Library Cataloguing in Publication Data

Stones, Rosemary
    Too close encounters and what to do about
    them. — (A Magnet book).
    1. Sexual harassment — Juvenile
    literature
    I. Title
    306.7   HQ23

    ISBN 0-416-03162-5

Too Close Encounters
and what to do about them

An essential book for teenagers that gives
straightforward, practical advice on how to
deal with all forms of sexual harassment and
abuse. Whether you want to know what to do
about raucous street comments, or where to
find help for more serious problems, the
answers are here.

For Catherine and Fred
with lots of love

Contents

Acknowledgements: Thanks to Catherine and Frederick Mann and their many friends for sharing experiences and ideas about teenage lives. Thanks also for information and advice to Inspector Sue Best of the Metropolitan police, Jo Bowyer of Dartington Social Research Unit, Louise Bradshaw of Pimlico School, Andrew Mann of South Bank Family Rights, Richie McMullen of Streetwise, Dr Gillian Mezey and Dr Michael King of the Institute of Psychiatry, Stockwell Women's Lift Service and John Vincent of Lambeth Amenity Services.

I Introduction

This book is about sexual harassment and sexual assault. At some point in their lives almost everyone suffers from some kind of unwanted sexual attention. This can be disturbing, frightening and, sometimes, dangerous. The more you know about different forms of harassment and assault the easier it will be for you to recognise the dangerous situations and devise strategies to cope with them. Perhaps you have been or are being sexually harrassed or assaulted, or you know someone who has suffered in this way. This book discusses these problems and what you can do about them and lists agencies that will be able to offer you advice and support.

As a teenager you can be particularly vulnerable. This is because:

1 You are an attractive young person with a sexually mature or almost sexually mature body

2 You probably go out a lot and are developing your friendships and interests

3 Your parents/guardians will no longer necessarily always know where you are and who you're with

4 You probably don't have much money for

11

things like a taxi home when you miss the last bus. Even if you're old enough to drive you may not be able to afford a car or even driving lessons. You're more likely to be walking home late at night and/or on your own.

When sexual assault or harassment is mentioned, people usually think of flashers or of rape, but there are other kinds too. It's important to know about all of them so that you can understand why some situations make you feel embarrassed and uncomfortable, recognise why other situations could be dangerous and know what steps you can take to protect yourself.

You and you alone have the right to control what happens to your body. No one should be allowed to:

1 Make you feel uncomfortable or embarrassed about your body
2 Touch you if you don't want to be touched
3 Coerce or bribe you into sexual activity that you are not sure about or don't want
4 Assault you for their sexual enjoyment
5 Misuse their authority to impose on you sexually.

And you, of course, do not have the right to do any of these things to other people.

II Strategies for the Protection and Control of Your Body

1. Educate Yourself About Sex

Knowledge is power, and if you are going to be in control of what happens to you as a sexual person, then your first step is to find out all you can about your body, about bodily changes and about sex.

Perhaps you have had sex education lessons at school. Your parents/guardians or friends may have given you information. It's sensible, though, to buy yourself a good sex education book. There are sure to be things that you were told when you were younger that didn't make much sense at the time and you will need to check them out again. You may have been given incorrect or out-of-date information about important things like contraception and sexually transmitted diseases. This is not a sex education book so I am not going to discuss these things here – but you must inform yourself about them. AIDS, for example, is a recent and frightening sexually transmitted disease and few sex education books have information on it. On page 109 of this book I list organisations that will provide leaflets and other information on it.

The best sex education book so far written for teenagers is *Make It Happy: What Sex is All About*

13

by Jane Cousins (Penguin ISBN 0 1400.5427 8). This is a paperback book and not expensive. If your nearest bookshop doesn't have it you can ask them to order it for you. On page 109 I list other sex education books that you might find useful. You may be able to get these from a library if you don't want to buy them.

Don't assume that a sex education book aimed at women and girls will be of no interest to a boy or one aimed at heterosexuals will have nothing to say to homosexuals. You will be spending the rest of your life communicating with, being friends with, perhaps loving people who are of the opposite sex or of a different sexual orientation to you. Part of caring about and respecting the rest of the human race is understanding and respecting *their* sexual feelings and needs; gaining such knowledge about others should be a part of your own sex education.

The sex education books that I have recommended will not only give you technical information about body changes and the mechanics of sex; they also discuss the context and the responsibilities of being a sexual person.

It's important to realise that sex and sexual feelings are not just about techniques and methods – how to do 'it'. They are about your whole body, your emotions, your identity, your values, the way you interact with other people, how you value yourself and how you value others.

You control your sexual feelings and needs and it is your right to be able to choose whether to act on them or not. Other people also have the right to
14

choose about their sexual needs and feelings. There is a big difference between a sexuality which respects others and cares that their sexual rights are not infringed and a sexuality that harasses, abuses, exploits or hurts others.

You are your body and as you grow to puberty you will find that you become preoccupied with intense sexual feelings. It happens to everyone, it's quite natural and it's very nice. It can sometimes be confusing and difficult to understand too. Sexual feelings are an expression of your changing emotional and spiritual being as well as your changing body. Sometimes it's helpful and reassuring to read about young people who are experiencing the sort of feelings and confusions about sex that you are experiencing. On page 110 I list some teenage novels that you may enjoy. None of the characters will be just like you but you will probably find some similarities.

If you're lucky enough to have a caring friend you can trust, then talking about your feelings and experiences together can also help.

2. Getting Adults to Help

Perhaps you get on very well with your parents/ guardians, are able to confide in them about lots of things including sexual matters and rely on them to help you even when you've done something silly or broken a family rule.

For some few teenagers, it's their own parents/ guardians or other family members who are actually a sexual danger to them, abusing them or sexually assaulting them. If this has ever happened to you or is happening at the moment turn to page 90 where I discuss this further and suggest organisations that will be able to support and help you. It is vital that you seek this help.

Most parents/guardians care desperately about their children, their safety and their happiness. They want to help but sometimes they don't know the best way to go about it. Some teenagers find it hard to tell their parents/guardians things and especially things to do with sex or sexual encounters. They think that if they do tell they will be shouted at and blamed for what has happened rather than helped.

> "There was this man who got on the same bus as me every day and used to stare at me in a sort of knowing way. It was creepy. I told my parents about him but all they did was go on about no wonder he stared with my skirt that length and why did I have to dress like that. I thought what's the use in telling them anything. All they do is have a go . . .'
> Parminder (13)

> 'When I started getting the obscene phone calls my mum was really suspicious, asking who I'd been going around with and everything. I'm sure she thought it was all my fault and I must have caused it to happen.'
> Maria (15)

Often parents/guardians who used to be understanding and gentle when you were little become nagging and bossy when you're a teenager. Home life, instead of feeling comfortable and relaxed starts to feel claustrophobic and restrictive. Of course parents/guardians find it hard to adjust to the fact that you're growing up and changing. They're used to laying down the law and they don't like it when you challenge them. But they are also frightened that some of the unpleasant or dangerous things that do happen to people – and in particular sexual assault – might happen to you.

Parents/guardians need reassurance. If they are at all approachable you might try introducing them to your friends – let them see for themselves what they're like. Try telling them where you're going and with whom and working out with them how you'll get home safely.

Perhaps your parents/guardians have already talked to you about their teenage days and their experiences of girlfriends/boyfriends, going to parties etc. If not, ask them – you'll be surprised how little you know about them, yet what happened to them as teenagers often affects the way they treat you as a teenager.

If your parents/guardians aren't approachable and just get angry and upset when you try and tell them things, then it might help if the subject of sexual harassment and assault and safety were tackled at your school. If your school has a number of sympathetic teachers or a council or parent/teacher organisation it might be possible to discuss

17

with them drawing up a *Charter for Adults to Help to Keep Teenagers Safe*. This Charter could then be sent to all parents for information and discussion. The Charter might be like this:

A Charter for Adults to Help to Keep Teenagers Safe

1 Adults (parents/guardians/teachers/doctors/ priests etc) should listen when a teenager tells them about being sexually harassed or assaulted and be prepared to believe her/ him.

2 Adults should say: 'I'm glad you told me'.

3 Adults should not blame the teenager for being sexually harassed or assaulted.

4 Adults should accept that a teenager who breaks family or school rules or takes silly risks does not deserve to be sexually harassed or assaulted and is not responsible for that harassment or assault. (If a rule has been broken that can be discussed and dealt with at some other time.)

5 Adults should tell teenagers that their safety is more important than anything else and that they are always prepared to help without getting angry and without prying.

6 Adults should work out safety strategies with teenagers so that if a teenager is ever in an uncomfortable or dangerous situation, s/he will immediately think of, eg:
   • phoning for adult help (reversing the

charges if necessary)
- asking to be met
- asking to be rescued from something s/he can't handle
- saying with confidence 'my mum/dad/ teacher/guardian knows where I am and is expecting me back now'.

7 Adults should decide with teenagers on a reliable fall-back person to whom the teenager can turn when they are not available.

Obviously not all teachers are approachable and not all will be well informed about sexual harassment and assault. You will know whether the Safety Charter idea is a good one for your school or not.

It must also be said that, in some rare instances, teachers or other adults in authority (eg priests, youth club leaders) are themselves guilty of sexually harassing or assaulting teenagers. This can be difficult to deal with because a place like a school is where adults tell you what to do and it's adults who make the rules.

Remember that adults are not always right. If an adult:
- asks you to do something that makes you uncomfortable or embarrassed
- asks you to keep that thing a secret
- asks you to undress (except for P.E. when the whole class is getting changed)

then you can refuse. You should also tell your parents/guardians or another teacher in whom you have confidence about what has happened.

If you have ever been sexually assaulted by a teacher or other adult in authority (however long ago) or if you are being assaulted now, then it's vital that you tell. If you can't tell your parents/guardians then turn to page 90 of this book which discusses sexual abuse by adults and lists organisations that will advise and help you.

Remember, if this is happening or has happened to you, that adult may also be assaulting other children or teenagers.

3. Everyone Needs Friends

Perhaps you are able to be very open with your parents/guardians about where you're going, what you're doing and who you're seeing, and you can rely on them to help to keep you safe while not interfering too much with your independence. If so that's great and you're lucky. If not you need to discuss the issue of safety with your best friends and devise ways in which you can help each other to keep safe.

It's important that someone who cares about you knows what's happening in your life – what's worrying you, who you're going out with, which club/pub/friend's house you go to. Then if something goes wrong, you have someone to rely on who knows where you might be and what you're up to, to help you get out safely.

'I was really bored Sunday so when this boy, who's much older than me, invited me round to his flat I went although I didn't know him very well and my mum would have gone mad if she'd known. I told my best friend where I was going and gave her the address and phone number just in case. As it happens, he did try it on and he got a bit nasty when I said no. Knowing Sandra had his details gave me the confidence to tell him that my mate knew where I was and was expecting me back. I got out of it all right.'
Sarah (15)

'My parents have this thing about hitch-hiking being dangerous even for boys, so I didn't tell them about thumbing to Newcastle. I told my friend Jason though and we arranged that I'd ring him when I got there. The idea was that if I didn't ring, at least he'd be able to tell the police where to start looking . . .'
Gideon (17)

If you are really determined to do something you know might get out of hand or be dangerous (as the people in the accounts above did) and you can't or won't tell your parents/guardians about it, then at least tell your best friend. Give her/him as much information as possible about where and with whom you will be, when you expect to be back and whom to tell (eg parents/guardians/police/teachers) if anything does go wrong.

And, before you do this foolish and dangerous thing, think again about whether you should do it at all. There is only one you.

Best friends are people you can confide in and share your thoughts and feelings with. You should be able to trust them not to make fun of you or let you down, and to care what happens to you. And you, of course, do the same for them.

But perhaps you haven't got a best friend. You may have moved house recently, you may live in a very isolated place, you may find it hard to make friends at all, let alone best friends.

Remember that making friends and staying friends is not something that just happens to us. There are few people who are so lovable and delightful to be with that they attract friends with no trouble at all. Most of us need to put some effort into making friends – we have to present our interesting and likeable qualities and demonstrate that we are interested in and concerned about other people too. If you're not meeting enough people it will be harder still to make friends. There are no magic wands to wave. You will have to solve this problem by developing your interests, joining in activities and so on.

I'm not suggesting that you need best friends just to help to keep you safe. We all need best friends all our lives for companionship and for sharing interests, experiences, love and affection.

Group Pressure
Friends will almost always play a good, positive

and supportive role in your life, but you must also be aware that the need for friendship and the desire to be part of a group or gang can sometimes lead people into going along with saying or doing cruel or evil things that they wouldn't dream of saying or doing if they were on their own.

Being different to everyone else in the gang or refusing to do something everyone else is doing can be difficult and painful and make you afraid that you will lose your friends. Sometimes a group or gang will use jeers and threats to make you go along with what they want to do ("He won't do it because he's queer"; "She's just frigid" etc).

One of the most horrible recent examples of group pressure occurred when two girls were raped by a gang of boys who took it in turns to hold them down. One boy whispered advice to one of the victims about what she might do to try and get the gang to let her go. This boy was obviously unhappy about what was going on but too afraid of the rest of the gang to oppose them openly and try and stop them.

When you go along with a group or gang in doing something that you wouldn't do as an individual you are avoiding taking responsibility for your actions. You pretend to yourself that what is happening isn't your fault, you didn't start it. This is a well-known feature of group or gang psychology.

These group/gang situations are hard to handle but it is always possible that if you are uncomfortable or shocked about something the group/gang is doing then some of the others may be too – perhaps they are too scared to say so. You could try appealing to the nicer people to support you in not taking part or stopping what is being done. If the situation is really out of hand you should not take part, saying why if you can. You might also try to leave or call for help.

You need to be aware of the dangers of group/gang psychology so that you can recognise it and avoid becoming a victim of it. As a member of a group or gang you must also be able to avoid being pressurised into going along with something that you will later regret and feel ashamed about.

4. Self-Preservation: Keeping Yourself Safe

When you're a teenager you often think that nothing bad can happen to you. You feel invulnerable. This sometimes means that you take risks – perhaps you hitch-hike, or walk home alone late at night, or go on blind dates, or get so high or so drunk that you don't know what you're doing. Usually teenagers do get away with it, but sometimes some don't.

In 1985, 578 incidents of rape or attempted rape and 1,939 cases of indecent assault were reported in the London Metropolitan district. It's impossible, though, to know how many sexual assaults actually happen as not everyone who is assaulted reports the crime to the police.

Some researchers think that five times as many rapes, for example, are committed as are
24

reported; some would put that figure even higher. In the United States it is estimated that one in four girls and one in ten boys will experience some kind of sexual assault as they grow up.

People who have been sexually assaulted sometimes feel too frightened or embarrassed to report what has happened. Sometimes they can't bear the thought of having to give all the details to a police officer and doctor. These days, in fact, the police are very much more aware of the feelings of people who have been sexually assaulted and they are trying to implement more sensitive and caring procedures for dealing with them.

If you have been sexually assaulted and you are too frightened or embarrassed to report what has happened, turn to page 86 of this book where I discuss what to do after such an attack and list organisations who will help and support you.

Sexual assaults can be very frightening and traumatic. Sometimes the after-effects linger on for a long time, affecting the victim's confidence, their feelings about sex and their trust in other people.

An important part of growing up is the development of your skills of self-preservation. Self-preservation is the ability to recognise dangerous situations and avoid them where possible and get out of dangerous situations safely if they can't be avoided.

Self-preservation is not just about going to self-defence classes or learning judo. Self-defence skills can be important (see the discussion on self-defence on page 27 of this book), but self-preservation is also about keeping alert and fit, taking safety precautions and trusting your instincts. If you feel uneasy about a person or a situation, you are probably right and you should take the appropriate self-preservation action.

Even if you decide to become a karate black belt there is no guarantee that you will *never* be sexually assaulted. Self-preservation skills *lessen* your chances of being assaulted.

Keeping Fit

Some people (particularly girls) start dropping out of sports and P.E. when they reach adolescence. Perhaps the choices offered at school aren't very interesting or sports activities are badly taught. Some girls are made to feel that it's not 'feminine' to be sporty and some boys who aren't very good at sport are made to feel that they're not macho enough. Both drop out so they won't be shown up.

Keeping fit is important, though, and if you don't enjoy sport or P.E. at school then you should try to organise some form of physical exercise for yourself (dancing, swimming, jogging, weight training, keep-fit exercises – anything!) on a regular basis. Not only is this good for your health and beauty, it also ensures that you're alert and in trim. Part of self-preservation is having a good idea of your physical capabilities – eg how fast you can move, how strong you are, how quick your reflexes are.

Say you find yourself in a dangerous situation in the street and you think you'll run for it. Could you realistically assess your chances of getting away?

When danger threatens adrenalin can help you to do things like run like hell, even if you're unfit – but it can't work miracles. Do you know how fast and how far you can run? Will you be puffed out by the time you reach the next lamp-post?

Self-Defence

Self-defence classes are now increasingly available. They are organised by women's groups, police volunteers, youth clubs and residents' associations and as adult education classes. Some schools also organise self-defence classes. Your local library should be able to help you find out if classes are available in your area.

If self-defence makes you feel more confident then that's good. When you feel confident you look confident and that in itself can often put off a would-be attacker.

But it is very important to be realistic about what you can achieve by doing a course in self-defence. Remember that:

1 Self-defence will not turn you into Wonder-woman or Superman and you must not start taking silly risks. There are sometimes dangerous situations (eg several attackers, an attacker with a gun or knife) that even a martial arts expert could not handle.

2 Self-defence techniques need to be *practised* regularly. It's no good going to a few classes and assuming that for the rest of your life you will be able to defend yourself. If they are not practised, your skills will rust.

3 However much self-defence training you have done, remember that an attack could happen when you're not on top form. We all get tired or ill from time to time.

4 Self-defence techniques should not be tested out unnecessarily. Do not deliberately walk into a dangerous situation so that you can try out your new skills. Do not, for example, over-react to verbal abuse by starting a fight.

5 If it is clear that your attacker is only interested in robbing you, then it may be safer to hand over your valuables. Do not risk being injured for the sake of a ring or purse.

6 In some situations it may be dangerous for you to try and defend yourself physically. Some very dangerous sexual attackers become more violent when a victim tries to fight back. There are others tactics – try talking your way out of it; try crying and screaming; some women and girls have pretended to be pregnant or to have their period or to have V.D. to try and put the attacker off. In the end, your life matters more than anything and in some situations it may be safer to submit to the attacker.

Perhaps you can't or don't want to go to self-defence classes. That's up to you but I think you would be sensible to at least consider the following:

1 If you can, run away, preferably towards a place where you know there will be people. It's always better to run if you can rather than

confront an attacker

2 Scream as loudly as you can. This may help to distract or scare off the attacker as well as summoning help

3 If you can't run away and your instinct is that fighting back may work, then fight with as much anger and dirtiness as you can manage. Try:

i: sticking your fingers in the attacker's eyes and clawing his/her face

ii: squeezing your attacker's windpipe

iii: kicking or kneeing your attacker (if male) in the balls

iv: kicking your attacker's shins

4 Do not worry about hurting your attacker. S/he has asked for it by attacking you

5 Run if you can as soon as you get the chance.

Defensive Weapons

If you are attacked you are legally entitled to defend yourself. But this does not mean that you are entitled to carry what the police term an 'offensive weapon' in order to do so. By this they mean objects such as a knife, a gun or a sharpened tool. If you carry a pepperpot about with you, intending to use it against an attacker, this could also be seen as an 'offensive weapon'.

But there are plenty of things that people naturally keep in their pockets and bags that you could use if you were attacked and which would not be seen as offensive weapons. A key, a pen or a metal comb can be jabbed into an attacker's face;

a bunch of keys can be used to strike the attacker. Hair spray can be sprayed into the attacker's eyes. (Don't waste precious minutes fumbling in your pockets or bag though!) An umbrella can be poked into an attacker's groin or solar plexus (the pit of the stomach) or used to hit the attacker. Of course you are allowed to carry a bleeper alarm, now available in a few hardware shops.

Safety at Home

Perhaps you live on your own, at college or with friends. Safety at home is something that you must take seriously. If you still live with your parents/ guardians and if you can, discuss safety at home with them. It's something they've probably thought about but it's worth making sure that they've considered the following safety points:

1 Your house/flat/bedsit should have strong door locks and preferably a dead bolt lock. Check the solidity of the door and frame at the point at which it is fitted. Windows should also be lockable. Accessible windows that you want to leave open should have bars.

2 It's sensible to install a peephole into your front door (and, if you're smaller than your guardians/parents, at a height that you can reach) so that you can see who is there before you open the door. You may also need a light outside the door that can be switched on from inside so that you can identify callers through the peephole when it's dark.

3 A door chain is also sensible. And don't feel

embarrassed to use it, particularly if you are on your own.

4 When it's dark draw curtains and blinds.

5 If you are a girl on your own, or if you live with just your mum, only your/her surname and initials should appear in the phone book and by your bell-push so that strangers don't know that there is a female living alone.

6 If a stranger calls and you need to go inside to fetch something (perhaps it's someone collecting for charity and you need to get your purse), always shut the door. I know it seems rude, but if you say something like: "Hold on a minute, I'll just get my purse," it's quite acceptable. (Besides your safety matters more than rudeness.)

7 Don't let strangers into the house unless you are sure that it's safe to do so. If someone comes to read the meter, for example, ask to see their identification (which they will have if they are genuine). This will be an official-looking card, probably with an attached photograph of the person. If you still feel uneasy, don't let them in.

8 Don't reveal to strangers, either at the door or on the phone, that you are alone in the house. Work out the sort of things you could say, eg "I'm afraid the others are a bit tied up at the moment. Can I take a message?"

9 Don't answer the phone by saying the phone number. If someone rings and asks what number they have called, ask *them* what

number they were trying to get and then say:
"Sorry. You've got a wrong number." (On
page 67 of this book, I discuss obscene phone
calls and what to do about them.)

10 If you come home alone and suspect that
your home has been broken into, don't go in.
The intruder may still be there. Go to a
neighbour or a phone box and call the police.

11 If you are in the house/flat/room and think
that someone has broken in, get out at once
and call the police. If you can't get out, try
and attract attention from a window; smash it
if necessary.

12 Don't give your key to anyone you don't
really trust.

13 As you approach your front door from the
street, have your key ready in your hand so
that you can open the door immediately and
get inside.

Safety When You Babysit

1 Don't babysit for strangers (perhaps you've
seen an ad in a newsagent's window, for
example) without checking them out first. If
possible ring them and if they sound OK
make an appointment to see them to discuss
possible babysitting. (If they are genuine *they*
will want to meet *you* before entrusting you
with their offspring.) Take a parent/guardian/
tough friend along with you. It's good that
they know that someone else knows who you
will be babysitting for and at what address.

2 When you are asked to babysit, make sure that you will be able to get home safely, especially if the people you're babysitting for plan to return very late. Will one of them drive you back or walk you to the bus stop?

3 Ask the people you are babysitting for to show you round the house before they go out. You need to be familiar with its lay-out.

4 Check with them before they leave that they have locked up securely, including the back door and accessible windows.

5 Make sure that you know where they are going and ask them to leave you a contact number if there is one.

6 Don't allow any stranger into the house while they are away unless they have told you to expect someone and described what s/he looks like.

7 If someone you don't know phones the people you are babysitting for, don't say: "I'm the babysitter" as this reveals that you are alone in the house with the children. Say, eg, "I'm sorry, Jane and Errol are busy at the moment. Can I take a message?"

Safety When Finding a Job

Whether you are looking for a Saturday job or for full-time employment, take sensible precautions. If you are applying to a well-known chain store with a personnel department, there are not likely to be dangers, but jobs are advertised in many different ways.

1 If you see an ad offering an astonishing amount of money for very little work (eg 'modelling'), it's likely to be dodgy. Don't go for an interview on your own.

2 Do not apply to escort agencies for a job, however tempting it may seem. Perhaps there are reputable escort agencies, but even these can't really vet their clients.

3 Check out especially carefully jobs advertised in newsagents or in the paper which don't give an address or company name.

4 If you go to a job agency, ask if they check out their clients. Do they, for example, make sure they really exist and at the address they have given? If it's a firm offering good money and perks for no qualifications, can they explain why?

5 If you take a job abroad, check out your employer before you go and make sure that you will be suitably and safely accommodated when you get there. Give your parents/guardians/best friends all the details about addresses, names etc before you leave.

Some careers, like social worker, doctor, estate agent, police officer, journalist, involve going on your own into strangers' houses. This can be particularly dangerous for women, although men have also, on occasion, been attacked. The recent disappearance of estate agent Susie Lamplugh has led to the setting up of the Susie Lamplugh Trust, which plans to investigate dangerous work situations for women and men and provide information and courses on keeping safe.

Safety in the Street and in Public Places

While it is everyone's right to be able to walk around unmolested at any time of the day or night in any public place, you should not imagine that simply putting this into practice ("Why shouldn't I walk home on my own at 2am?") will make other people respect it and leave you alone.

Part of the process of becoming an independent person is being able to appreciate the difference between what *should* happen in society and what actually *does* happen. Sexual harassment and sexual assaults *do* happen.

Of course you can decide that this is unfair and think about ways that society might be changed, if you want to. You might decide to join a local residents' group, or women's group or youth club for example. Campaigning for better local transport services, women-only lift services, more police on the beat or better street lighting are some of the practical ways that streets and public places could be made safer. Tackling the reasons why sexual attacks happen in the first place is a much more difficult and long term prospect and I discuss this further on page 54 of this book.

1 If you can, avoid walking home late on your own or in unsafe areas. If you have no alternative, try to walk quickly and confidently, keeping to well-lit streets. Walk

on the side of the pavement nearest the road to avoid dark doorways.

2 Get to know the routes you usually have to travel – where there are concealed entrances, where the lighting is bad, where there are pubs or garages or public phones. Familiarity with your surroundings will make it easier for you to avoid danger spots and know where you might be able to get help if you needed it.

3 Make sure you have the right change in your pocket for the bus/train/tube/phone. It's also a good idea to have a phone card on you.

4 If you think that you are being followed, trust your instincts and take action. As confidently as you can, cross over the road, turning as you do so so that you can see whoever is behind you. If possible go into a shop/pub/restaurant and ask for help. If there are people around, approach a group that includes women and ask them to help you. If none of that is possible, walk as confidently as you can up to the front door of a house that looks occupied (perhaps there are lights on) and ring the bell.

5 Beware of a stranger who warns you of the dangers of walking alone and offers to accompany you. This is a ploy attackers sometimes use.

6 Have your key ready in your pocket so that you can let yourself into your home quickly.

7 If you know that you are in no fit state to get

get home safely on your own (perhaps you are drunk, or your clothes are so fashionably tight you can hardly move) then try to get a friend to accompany you or take a taxi or phone home to be picked up. Remember that it's better to lose face than to put yourself in danger.

8   If you are waiting for a bus/tube/train at night, try to wait in a well-lit place, near groups of people, preferably including women. When you get on the bus/tube/train, try to sit near groups of passengers or near the driver/conductor/guard.

9   If you sense that you might be harassed by someone, try making yourself as repulsive as possible eg by picking your nose, scratching, or muttering to yourself in a crazy way.

10 If you find yourself alone in a train/tube carriage with someone who makes you feel uneasy, get out at the next stop and change carriages.

11 If you are bothered by a stranger in a bus/tube/train or in a public place, don't hesitate to take action. Change your seat or move away. Say in a loud, indignant voice "Do you mind!"/"This man is bothering me!" etc.

12 Beware of a stranger who asks you where you are going or at which stop you are getting off.

13 If you are a girl, check whether there is a women-only lift service in your area. Your local library should be able to help you.

Hitch-hiking

It is not safe to hitch-hike and you shouldn't do it unless there is no other alternative.

Of course, cuts in transport services, particularly in rural areas, mean that for some people there is no alternative to hitching; there are no night buses for them any more and sometimes no buses at all. Constant rises in the price of, for example, train tickets, are putting safe travel on public transport out of many people's reach.

These cuts and price rises are a safety issue and should be considered part of any campaign to improve safety on the streets and in public places.

If you really have to hitch, be particularly alert and follow these safety precautions:

1 Must you hitch? Try to make plans in advance and find another way to travel – could you and your friends get together to organise shared mini-cabs, for example?

2 Never hitch alone. If you're a girl, it's safer to hitch with a boy.

3 Do not accept a lift from someone you don't like the look of. You may feel embarrassed about refusing a lift once they have stopped for you, but instincts are often right. Your safety is what matters.

4 It's safer to try and get a lift in a well-lit public place like a garage or motorway service-station. You will have a chance to size up suitable motorists and ask them for a lift. Always approach women drivers or a woman and man, if you can. Never ask two or more

men in a car for a lift. Lorry drivers with company names on their lorries are a reasonable bet – they have schedules and professional reputations to keep.

5 It's difficult to be choosy about different types of cars when you need a lift, but try not to accept a lift which will involve sitting in the back of a two-door car.

6 Keep any luggage you have on your knee if you can.

Safety When Driving

1 When you're driving on your own, make sure the passenger door is locked. Some people like to lock the driver's door too; others prefer to leave it unlocked in case they need to get out quickly in an accident. Whichever feels safer is right for you.

2 Close all windows and lock the car when you leave it. Try to park in a well-lit public place.

3 When you return to the car, have your car keys ready in your hand. Before you get in, check there's no one hiding in the back.

4 If you have to wait in the car in a dodgy area, lock the doors from the inside and wind the windows up till they're nearly shut.

5 Don't give lifts to hitchers. If you really must, only give lifts to girls/women.

6 If you think you're being followed, drive to a police station, garage, or other busy public place and ask for help.

7 Keep a torch in the car so that if you break down you can check your surroundings.
8 Learn how to change a wheel so that you don't have to approach strangers to help you.
9 Save up and join the AA or RAC so that if you break down you can phone for reliable, prompt (fairly!) assistance.

III Sex and Society: Some Problematic Areas

1. The Messages of Dress

You have the right to wear whatever you want without being sexually harassed or sexually assaulted. Just as you have the right to walk the streets without being molested, but in real life you know that you have to take sensible precautions when you go out, so you have to think seriously about what kind of messages your clothes are conveying to people, what kinds of reactions they will have – and whether you can handle them.

There are a lot of unwritten laws about the ways we dress and they're often confusing. There's not a lot of real difference, for example, between wearing a bikini on the beach and undressing to reveal bra and pants – yet the bikini is seen as OK and the bra and pants as shocking. These unwritten laws about dress are generally agreed by society although they're not always very rational. If you break them you have to be sure that you can handle people's reactions.

Consciously or unconsciously, people choose clothes (and make-up and jewellery) to send out messages about their social status, their culture, their social and political attitudes – and their sexuality. (Money allowing, of course.) Learning to decode these messages about dress can be interesting and entertaining.

Some groups in society like gay men, for example, may use a distinctive way of dressing to identify themselves to each other, as well as to assert their gayness. If you live in a city with a sizeable gay community, you will probably have already learnt to recognise this style.

When you're trying out different dress styles you may find that, without meaning to, you're giving out the 'wrong' message:

> *'I really wanted this black leather gear I saw in a shop and I imagined myself parading down the Kings Road in it of a Saturday. When I told my mum she said did I know it was a gay men's fashion. I'd never realised before she said it.'*
> Joshua (13)

> *'I liked the mini-skirt when I tried it on in the shop, although it was on the micro rather than mini side. But at the disco boys kept saying all these disgusting things to me. I never wore it after.'*
> Michele (15)

You should also be realistic about the different responses to dress messages that people from different cultures or of different ages may have. Older people may be shocked by what they see as sexual messages in dress that younger people take for granted.

If you go abroad to a country where dress conventions are different, it can be dangerous (as well as discourteous) to wear clothes that give out messages which in that culture are seen as sexual. In the Gulf States, for example, bare arms for girls/ women are not acceptable. You should be able to work out a style of dress which you feel happy in, that is not sending out the 'wrong' messages.

Although you may not intend it, it could be that your style of dress and appearance is frightening and intimidating. The 'message' being sent out may be an aggressively sexual one.

Groups such as male punks, roughnecks and skinheads, especially when they crowd other people on the pavement or hang around bus and tube stations, may not realise quite how frightening they are, especially to girls and women on their own. If that's your style, then make sure your behaviour is sensitive and non-threatening.

2. Privacy and Nudity

As teenagers approach puberty and their bodies begin to develop and change, they often feel the need for more privacy.

Perhaps you're lucky enough to have your own bedroom. But even if you haven't, you can work out rules that will allow your privacy and personal space to be respected, and you to respect the privacy and personal space of the people you live with. Knocking before you go into someone's bedroom is a good rule; so is allocating reasonable time in the bathroom so that you can bath in peace but at a time convenient for everyone else.

Periods or wet dreams mean that from time to time your sheets and underwear will be stained. There needs to be a relaxed way for you to be able to wash them or put them for washing and have access to clean things.

Our society is confused about nudity and different people have different attitudes to it. Some people wander around at home in the nude and it's all quite relaxed and comfortable without any embarrassing or sexual overtones. On some beaches nudity is also acceptable these days. If you feel safe and comfortable about it, that's fine. As you get older you may feel the need for more privacy even if your parents/guardians wander around in the nude. Do what feels right for you. Other people wouldn't dream of being seen without their clothes and feel embarrassed about bodies. That's right for them.

Whatever your state of dress or undress no one has the right to sexually assault you in any way whatsoever. But obviously you must be alert to the different connotations that different people put on nudity. Are they relaxed and comfortable about it, or do you detect sexual overtones that make you uneasy? If you're abroad and you want to sunbathe or swim in the nude, check out whether that's acceptable or not before you do it.

3. Your Sexual Needs and Your Safety

Not everyone is interested in sex – some people live very happy lives without it. Other people are interested. If you're one of them you will, at your own pace, become sexually ready and want to have sexual experiences.

It's not always easy though. Mr or Ms Right will not necessarily be around when you want them to be, or if they are, will not necessarily be interested in you. Sometimes the build-up of sexual tension and desire that you will experience can feel almost unbearable and you may be tempted to enter into a sexual relationship with someone who is available but who, in your cooler moments, you know to be quite the wrong person for you – perhaps even an untrustworthy or dangerous person. Sexual need can make you vulnerable to exploitation and hurt by small-minded or unscrupulous people you'd normally steer clear of.

The sensible solution is self-help – masturbation. It's normal and natural and when you haven't got the right sexual partner around for you, it's the obvious and safe answer.

Both girls and boys masturbate. It's a natural part of sexual self-exploration – a way of discovering and satisfying your own sexual responses. You will find information about masturbation in the sex education books listed on page 109 of this book.

Sex is not always about satisfying a sexual partner – although that is often how it is presented to us. Masturbation is not second-rate or stop-gap

45

sex; it's just different sex. Enjoy it and value it as a sexual experience in its own right. You'll probably find that throughout your sexual life you'll masturbate from time to time – perhaps you won't want to be involved with anyone, your partner may be away or ill or your sexual drive may be stronger than your partner's.

4. Fantasy

Part of becoming a mature sexual person is having dreams and fantasies about sex. This is quite normal.

You may find that you dream or fantasise about people you know, although in real life you wouldn't have any kind of sexual relationship with them. You may find that your dreams or fantasies involve rape or being raped, forcible sex, sex with more than one person, sex with some glamorous stranger. You may even dream or fantasise about sex with your own relatives, for example, your parents, sisters or brothers.

All this is quite common. There is no sexual dream or fantasy that you have that lots of other people have not also had. What you should remember is that you control your dreams and fantasies and you can change them or end them if they make you feel uncomfortable. This is not true of real-life sexual assaults.

Such dreams or fantasies do *not* mean that in real life you want to be raped or to commit incest, or any
46

of the things that you might fantasise or dream about.

If you have such dreams or fantasies and you are then the victim of a sexual assault or incest in real life, do not imagine that you are therefore to blame, that you 'really' wanted it to happen. There is no automatic connection between your sexual dreams and fantasies and real-life sexual violence.

There is a small number of people (usually male) who have persistent fantasies that centre on the violent aspects of rape or other sexual attacks. There does appear to be a connection between fantisies such as these and actual sexual attacks. New therapy techniques have helped some of these people to change their fantasies (and also their behaviour) to more 'normal' reciprocal sexual fantasies. If you are worried about violent sexual fantasies, turn to page 62 of this book when I discuss tendencies to sexual violence and what to do about them.

5. Sex and Money

As with many things to do with sex, our society is confused about the relation between sex and money, between sexual attraction and the power that money can buy. Advertisements for sports cars, expensive alcohol, perfumes and clothes all suggest that ownership of the right consumer goods will make you sexually attractive. They also suggest that people who have these things *are* sexually attractive.

It's important that you learn to distinguish between people's intrinsic qualities (sense of humour, spontaneity, wit, gentleness, reliability, loyalty, generosity) and their 'trappings' – how stylishly they are dressed, what kind of car/ motorbike they drive, how rich their parents are or how big their house is. Of course there is a link – it's a lot easier, for example, to be spontaneous and generous when you've money in your pocket, the right clothes to wear and a car to drive around in. But however rich or poor someone is, the basic qualities will be there that will attract you or not.

Sometimes it's tempting to go out with someone you're not at all keen on because they can afford to take you somewhere nice and buy you treats. If you know that's what you're up to and they know it too, and accept it, that's fine because you're both playing the same (rather tacky) game. Beware though of being pressurised or feeling obliged to take part in sexual activity that you don't want in return for these treats. Just because someone's bought you prawn cocktail and a medium steak, it doesn't mean that they have the right to expect sexual favours. Nor, of course, should you ever expect sexual favours in return for shelling out on presents, evenings out, candlelit dinners etc. Sex should not be a commercial transaction.

But of course, sex sometimes is very much a commercial transaction – call-girls, prostitutes and rent-boys sell sex for money; models are paid to pose topless for newspapers. People are paid to
48

work in pornographic films and for pornographic magazines.

Some teenagers – boys as well as girls – get caught up in this dangerous world of sex for money. There can be many reasons – perhaps your home life is unbearable and sex with strangers offers you affection and comfort of a sort and makes you feel needed; perhaps you think of it as an easy way to make money; perhaps you desperately need money because you're hooked on drugs; perhaps you've left home and can't make ends meet.

Remember that receiving money or presents for sex is prostitution – it is using sex in a commercial way. But if you have done this or are doing it, it does not mean that you are now a prostitute or a rent-boy and always will be. There is plenty of time for you to think about why you are doing what you are doing and get out of it. On page 106 of this book I list agencies who will help and support you to take the right steps. If drug dependency is a part of your problem, there are agencies to help with this too.

And you *must* get out of it. Selling sex is extremely dangerous. Teenagers who do it risk murder, brutal assault, torture, being drawn into pornography, catching sexually transmitted diseases including AIDS, and possible future difficulties in relating sexually to someone they love. Girls also run the increased risk of cervical cancer later in life.

6. Pornography

Sex is a natural part of life and since works of art are about life, sex and sexual feelings have for centuries been the subject matter of paintings, sculpture, poems, novels and more recently films and photographs. This kind of art is called erotic art and it is a celebration of sexuality and sexual feelings.

Pornography is an extreme form of erotic art. It is often difficult to be clear in what way erotic art is different from pornography because people who disapprove of any kind of frank depiction of nudity or sexuality in art tend to call all such overt material 'pornographic'.

However, there is a difference between erotic art which celebrates sex and sexual feelings and pornography which is material simply intended to make you feel horny. The people shown in pornographic material (usually magazines and films) are presented as sexual objects, in gymnastic or gynaecological poses.

Many people object to pornography because it often links sex and violence and presents women as enjoying sexual violence. Some hardcore pornography presents illegal sexual activity (eg sex with under-age children or with animals).

Some people think that pornography is necessary for people who want to be sexually aroused but who don't have, or don't want to have, a sexual partner. Others think that there is a link between hardcore pornography (which often depicts violent sexual attacks) and sexual attacks in real life. On the other hand, some feminists think that it should be possible to produce sexually exciting material that does not degrade women.

Soft-core pornographic magazines, books and films are easily available these days – to older teenagers too. They can be a useful source of information as well as sexually arousing, as long as you realise that, eg, in magazines the glamorous photographs of young, slim models are touched up with air brushes – no one looks as good as that in real life. There are now soft-core magazines aimed at heterosexual girls and women with photographs of nude men, and soft-core magazines aimed at gays and lesbians although these are not widely available.

If you buy this kind of material, it's important not to use it to sexually harass other people who may feel embarrassed or threatened by it. Girls and women, in particular, are already surrounded by pictures of half-dressed and undressed women on hoardings and in newspapers and can feel very vulnerable at seeing a crowd of boys sniggering over a porn magazine. You should also be aware that this material presents a very misleading and sexist view of sexuality.

The wider world of pornography – sex shops, strip clubs, massage parlours, escort agencies, prostitution – is a dangerous world that you should not be tempted to get involved in. Beware of jobs offering very good money for 'modelling' or being an 'escort'. However much you like someone, do

51

not allow them to photograph you in the nude.

7. Running Away From Home

When your home life is intolerable it is tempting to think of running away as a solution to your difficulties. But running away can in itself be very dangerous. If you leave home you will almost certainly find yourself homeless and without money. You may be vulnerable to approaches from pimps and others who will offer food and warmth in return for sexual services.

You should consider what it is about your home life that's so bad. If you are being sexually or physically abused then there is no question about it – you must tell. Once you have told and been believed, machinery will be set in motion to remove you from danger and keep you safe; perhaps you will be taken into care, or be able to stay with another, non-abusing relative or with a friend. On page 90 I discuss abuse in the home and list agencies who will help and support you.

If your family life is intolerable because of tension and rows, you should consider to what extent this is due to your parents/guardians' anxiety about you as a teenager and what your role is in this. If things are really bad, family therapy or counselling might be considered; your doctor will be able to advise on this. If you're an older teenager, remember that you will probably be leaving home soon anyway, when you start college or if you get a job – it may be sensible just to stick it out.

Whatever you do, don't run away from home unless you have somewhere and someone (eg a trusted friend or relative) to run to. And if you do run away, at least let your parents/guardians know that you are safe. The Salvation Army will pass on messages from runaways without revealing their whereabouts. On page 108 is a list of organisations that offer advice and help to runaways.

IV Why Do Sexual Harassment and Sexual Assault Happen?

Both girls and boys, women and men can be victims of sexual harassment or sexual assault – but almost all attacks are carried out by men – both attacks on girls and women and attacks on boys and on other men.

Some kinds of sexual harassment, like obscene phone calls or flashing, are thought to be carried out by people (again almost always men) who are in some way inadequate. These kinds of harassment (discussed in more detail on page 67) can be frightening and annoying but they are very rarely dangerous.

Other kinds of sexual harassment (eg bum pinching) and sexual assault (eg rape) can be carried out by inadequate people, but they are also carried out by people who are not 'inadequate' but who are considered perfectly 'normal'. We need to ask why such people do it and whether we can change society so that sexual harassment and sexual assault do not occur.

1. Sex Stereotyping

The reasons for sexual harassment and sexual assault, and in particular the fact that girls and women are almost always the victims and boys and men almost always the perpetrators, are deeply embedded in the way our society sees the roles of women and men, girls and boys.

Every society, as far as we know, has different ideas of what is appropriate behaviour for girls and women and what is appropriate behavious for boys and men, over and above the obvious biological differences. These different expectations are not inherent – there is no biological reason, for example, for males to cry less than females. It's just that boys in our society are taught from babyhood that crying is not 'masculine' and they shouldn't do it. There is no biological reason for females to be less good at science than males – it's just that until very recently girls have been made to feel that science is a man's subject; they have also not been given equal opportunities with boys to take it up.

In the past, conventional thinking about the place of girls and women in our society was that they were naturally inferior to males. Don't forget that women in Britain only got the vote in 1918. In the last century women were even seen as the property of a man – first as a daughter and then as a wife. Anne Brontë, one of the famous Brontë sisters (her sister Charlotte wrote *Jane Eyre* and her sister Emily *Wuthering Heights*) published a novel called *The Tenant of Wildfell Hall* in 1848. It tells of the plight of a woman married to a violent drunkard, Arthur Huntingdon, who has no escape because, on marriage, all her money and property automatically became her husband's. This was the actual legal position for women at the time. The gradual changing of laws to do with property and inheritance has been of fundamental importance in changing the status of women in our society.

As women have become increasingly independent, they have broken away from the domestic worlds of the family and the home and taken their place in the larger world. This has not 'caused' sexual harassment and assault to happen (they always did) but it has meant that women have begun to speak out about sexual violence and protest about it. Because society has been made to take the issue of sexual violence against women seriously (although still not seriously enough), it has now become possible to talk about other kinds of sexual violence, including sexual violence against children and young people.

Our thinking in general about sexuality is unfortunately still influenced by the past rather than by the social, economic and technological changes that have altered society's expectations of female and male behaviour. Although sex is much discussed these days (sex education lessons in school, for example), because of its private nature, it remains at the same time a secret, hidden part of our lives. This makes it harder for us to work out a new language of sexuality that does not see girls and women as sex objects, as whores or 'good' girls, and boys and men as aggressive sexual initiators, as 'studs' or 'wimps'.

Our society is particularly confused about the difference between normal healthy sexuality and sexual violence. Conventionally, in a heterosexual relationship, the boy is supposed to initiate sexual activity and 'persuade' or 'cajole' the girl to go along with it. This leaves lots of room for mis-understandings. How do you tell the difference between someone signalling "I really like you and want to get to know you better" or "I'd like to kiss and cuddle with you" or "I'd like to sleep with you"? The language of sexual attraction and sexual activity can be explicit but it is more likely to be a mixture of eye contact, body language and hints, especially if either party is sexually inexperi-enced, uncertain about the other person's real feelings, or afraid of being rejected. There is a subtle but crucial difference, which some people never learn between 'persuading' and *forcing*, 'cajoling' and *coercing* the other person into sexual activity.

The way that sexual activity and sexual attraction are constantly linked with violence – in films, on television and in books – suggests that sexual violence is somehow OK, perhaps rather enjoyable. A teenage novel published recently in Britain even described the teenage heroine having an orgasm as she is raped by the pop star she has just met. Later in the book she marries him. This is a blatant example of the 'she-wanted-it-really' myth that is used to excuse sexual violence against women and girls.

It's true that some people find violence sexy – but the violence they enjoy is a *fantasy* violence that they have control over. It has nothing to do with the

57

reality of the feelings of violation and exploitation that are suffered by victims of sexual assault. Don't forget that rape and sexual humiliation are used as forms of torture by régimes round the world that practise torture.

These days things are gradually changing – at least for young people. You've probably done work at school on stereotyping and are aware of the pressures on teenagers to conform to sex-role expectations – the boys-must-push-for-sex/girls-must-resist-sex syndrome.

Boys are beginning to evolve a way of behaving that allows them to show their feelings and be gentle and caring rather than always pretending to be macho hard men. Girls are becoming more confident and assertive about their needs and feelings in relationships. Lots of teenagers these days share expenses or take turns at treating each other on dates, rather than always expecting the boy to pay. In its small way, this shows how teenagers can share and take equal responsibility in a relationship.

Of course this doesn't mean that if you fancy someone, you can't show it or do anything about it. Seduction techniques are fine if they involve showing positive liking and admiration, perhaps backed up by friendly gestures that signal "I fancy you" eg 'happening' to be walking the same way, nice remarks and chat, getting your friends to drop hints for you and so on.

Emotional pressuring ('I'll kill myself if you don't go out with me'), bribery or force of any kind are not acceptable seduction techniques.

2. Sexual Good Manners

Everyone deserves to be well treated and not to have their self-esteem hurt. Sometimes you don't realise that you are hurting the other person, or you feel poorly treated and you're not sure why. What is needed very often are simple good sexual manners; by this I mean behaviour that respects other people's sexual rights and does not set out to exploit or demean them:

1 Do not assume that your girl/boyfriend is exactly like you, with precisely the same needs and feelings. Take time to get to know her/him and learn to respond to her/his needs and feelings. It's called sharing and it's a lovely thing to do.

2 You don't have to have sex to have a good relationship with your girl/boyfriend.

3 Do not pressurise your girl/boyfriend into sexual activity by making her/him feel bad ('You don't love me enough') or by threatening her/him ('There's plenty of other girls/boys I can go out with if you won't do it').

4 You do not have to have sex to prove you love your girl/boyfriend. If it doesn't feel comfortable and good to go ahead with sexual activity, then don't.

5 Do not take advantage of your girl/boyfriend's ignorance about sex to push her/

him into going further than s/he really wants to.

6 Do not take sexual advantage of your girl/boyfriend if s/he is too drunk or too high to know what's going on.

7 Do not reveal intimate details about your girl/boyfriend to the world. It's cruel and shows that you are untrustworthy. Sexual activity is private.

8 Do not expect sexual favours in return for spending money on someone (eg taking her/him out to dinner).

9 If you know that your girl/boyfriend has slept with someone before, do not assume that s/he must therefore sleep with you. What happened before is none of your business.

10 If you have slept with someone once, that doesn't mean that you're obliged to keep on sleeping with that person, or obliged to sleep with anyone else if you don't want to. Saying yes once doesn't commit you to always saying yes.

11 If you're genuinely not sure whether your girl/boyfriend means what s/he says when s/he says no to sexual activity, then you can ask again in a different way. Say, for example, 'I know sometimes people think they have to say no to sex but they really want to say yes. Is that what you're doing now?' If the answer is still no then accept it and do not try to pressure your girl/boyfriend to change her/his mind

12 Just because someone's attracted to you
   doesn't mean that you are in any way
   sexually obliged to them. Say no.
13 If you've slept with someone it doesn't mean
   that you're tied to her/him for life. Bonds are
   created by sex but don't allow yourself to
   feel trapped by what may have been a
   mistake. Remember, you have the rest of
   your life to live.

3. How To Say No

Funnily enough, it's often hard to say no.

Some people's parents/guardians behave in a
distant, rather authoritarian way, laying down rules
rather than discussing things and airing different
points of view. This means that the teenager
involved gets used to doing as s/he is told rather
than thinking things out for her/himself. S/he is
certainly not used to saying no, particularly to
adults. Schools of course, tend to work in the same
way as authoritarian parents.

Girls are conventionally expected to be 'nice'
and if they say no they are often told that they are
being 'aggressive' and behaving in a way that's not
'feminine'. They get discouraged from coming
straight out with how they feel and think they have
to mask it in a 'nice' way so as not to hurt other
people's feelings.

Some sex education books (invariably those
written by men) go on about how frail the male ego

61

is and how important it is that girls/women do not make men feel sexually rejected (they might get impotent). This is a very convenient argument for men 'needing' to get their own way sexually. The best place for sex education books that put forward such nonsense is the bin.

Practise saying no. Think of situations that you don't like or don't want – eg friends at school always borrowing your pens without giving them back; your little brother always getting out of the washing up. Speak up for yourself and see how it goes. If you get good at saying no about small things you don't like you'll be able to cope with saying no about more important things.

Now think how you would say no in a sticky dating situation. If you are a girl there is the double standard to cope with ('girls-say-no-when-they-mean-yes'). Indicate clearly that no means no – look the person in the eye and say no as firmly and confidently as you can. You can also use body language – straighten up, stiffen and move back.

And remember, if someone says no to you, it's not the end of the world. Perhaps s/he will say yes when and if your relationship develops further. If not, there are other fish in the sea. Rejection is part of the process of finding the right person for you.

4. A Tendency to Sexual Violence

Although there are no definite personality clues to look out for that will reveal whether a person is likely to commit sexual assault, there are ways of behaving which are not just uncaring but which exploit other people. Perhaps we've all done one or two of these nasty things in our worse moments, but watch out for someone who:

1 is extremely self-centred and not interested in other people's needs and feelings

2 gets angry or sulky when s/he doesn't get her/his own way

3 manipulates people to get her/his own way using emotional pressure or bribery

4 is convinced that s/he has a right to always get what s/he wants

5 exploits other people's sense of decency and trust

6 makes sexual jokes which reveal contemptuous attitudes to females/males

7 treats her/his girl/boyfriend as a sex object rather than as a person

8 is excessively jealous and possessive, always supposing that her/his girl/boyfriend fancies someone else

9 belittles her/his girl/boyfriend in public by ignoring her/him or flirting with someone else

10 has sexual relationships with girls/boys from a different social class/ethnic group because s/he thinks they are inferior and when s/he would not dream of having a sexual relationship with someone from their own class/group

11 has sexual relationships with girls/boys from a different social class/ethnic group in order

to 'revenge' her/himself on that class/group.

Among the teenagers of today there are undoubtedly some who will commit or are already committing acts of sexual violence or sexually harassing people. Perhaps they are making obscene phone calls, running up to women and touching their breasts, masturbating on trains and buses or actually attacking people.

Such teenagers sometimes find that, while they have difficulty making friends and especially girl / boyfriends, their sex fantasies are increasingly about committing sexual violence.

Some of these teenagers know that there is something wrong with their behaviour and it worries them. This is a very good sign because it means that they are aware that their actions frighten and hurt other people and that they are responsible for those actions.

Those teenagers (and older people who behave in this way) need help and it's important that they get it. There is some evidence that people who behave in a sexually deviant way (touching, obscene phone calls etc) can progress to actual sexual attacks.

> *'I was masturbating on the buses. I would sit myself upstairs behind a group of girls and do it. I knew there was something wrong but I couldn't help it. I didn't know where to go so in the end I went to a VD clinic and told them.'*
> Simon (now 23)

64

If you are worried about your sexual behaviour, seek help. There are counsellors and therapists who will be able to help you understand and work at changing your behaviour. It's not always easy to get the right help but you should start by explaining things to your doctor and asking her/him to refer you for appropriate help. If you feel very desperate and alone, ring the Samaritans. You will find the number in the phone book.

5. Alcohol and Drugs

Some researchers have found that a large number of sexual attacks have been committed by people who have been drinking. Alcohol and some drugs have the effect of lowering our inhibitions. If someone has a tendency towards sexual violence it's possible that too much alcohol or stimulant will push them to commit sexual violence.

Beware of the effect of alcohol/drugs on you and don't let yourself do something that you will regret the next day when you have a clearer head.

V Sexual Harassment, Assault and Abuse

1. Reporting Sexual Harassment

'I was coming down the escalator in Selfridges when this man walked straight up to me, smiling, and put his hand on my breast. I swore at him; there didn't seem much else I could do.'
Marcia (16)

'It was in the station tunnel. I wasn't sure which platform and I was trying to work it out when a boy came up to me and suddenly put his hand up my skirt and touched my thigh. He said: 'Don't tell anyone' and ran off. I was amazed rather than frightened.'
Miranda (14)

If someone touches you in a sexual way in a crowded shop, or you get an obscene phone call, or you are flashed, it sometimes doesn't seem worth telling anyone about it, much less reporting it to the police. After all, there's not much the police can do to trace the offender. And perhaps you don't feel particularly upset or bothered by the incident. That's fine and it's good if you feel confident.

You should bear in mind, though, that there are other reasons for reporting sexual harassment. Most importantly, *you* may not have felt threatened and upset by what happened but perhaps the next victim will – it could be a child or a woman who has recently been raped and is feeling very vulnerable. It could be that the man in the shop (in the incident described above) makes a habit of touching female customers and if you report the incident to the management they will keep an eye out for him. Reporting incidents to the police, even if they can't do anything about what has happened, helps to give them a clearer picture of how widespread sexual harassment is.

Also, however cool and collected you may feel about what has happened, it's important to tell someone about it even if you don't report it formally. If you tell your parents/guardians/best friends, you will find it helps you to put the incident in perspective.

2. Obscene Phone Calls

> *'He rang every Saturday at about midnight. Quite a young, pleasant voice. He'd start talking about my legs and how he liked to imagine doing this and that with me. I just put the phone down but when it continued I got a man friend to answer. He stopped after a while.'*
> Beverley (18)

Very little is known about the people (invariably

male) who make obscene phone calls; they are by definition hard to catch. The calls can vary from the faintly titillating ('What colour panties are you wearing?') to the terrifyingly obscene mixed with violent threats.

Obscene phone calls can be very frightening, especially if you're alone in the house. There's always the fear at the back of your mind that the caller might know your address from the phone book and appear at the door.

Some obscene phone callers start by trying to get you to tell them your name, or pretend they are a friend, and ask you to guess who they are. Don't be tempted to play this game. If they won't tell you who they are, don't give them your name, and put the phone down.

Psychiatrists think that obscene phone callers are lonely, inadequate people who probably masturbate as they make the calls. They are not usually dangerous and there does not appear to be any immediate link between obscene phone calls and actual attacks. Here are some tactics for dealing with obscene phone calls:

1 Tell your parents/guardians/best friends/ flat-mates about it. You need moral support and practical help.

2 Try to arrange for a man to answer the phone until you're sure the caller is discouraged.

3 If you're feeling really confident (and can keep from laughing) pretend that the line is bad and you can't hear what's being said. (Nothing is more frustrating for the obscene

phone caller.) Say, 'Sorry you'll have to speak up, this is a bad line. No, sorry I just can't hear you,' and so on.

4 Buy a mountain rescue whistle from a sports shop that sells climbing gear and blow it into the phone as loud as you can.

5 Report the calls to the police. If they are very disturbing you can ask British Telecom to arrange to have your calls intercepted. This means that only calls from people you have named will be put through to you. You might also consider getting your number changed and going ex-directory.

6 If you live on your own and you're now feeling nervous, arrange for a rota of trusted friends to stay until you get your confidence back. Don't feel shy about this – obscene phone calls are frightening and it's not surprising if you feel a bit shaky.

3. Flashing

'My mate and me were eating our sandwiches in the park when this man appears from behind a tree. He was holding his thing out and shouting at us to look.'
Glenys (13)

'I was in a bookshop and quite engrossed in looking through some shelves. This oldish man was standing next to me and I got a sort of feeling. I glanced sideways and he'd got

*his fly open and his penis showing. It was all
shrivelled up and small like a gherkin, I
thought.'*
Maggie (16)

Flashers are people (usually men but sometimes
women) who expose their genitals in public. It is
thought that they are inadequates who like to
surprise their victims by displaying themselves.
They later use the incident to fantasise around in
private for sexual satisfaction. 95% of male flashers
expose with a limp penis (ie they don't have an
erection that makes their penis stick out) and they
are not dangerous – they will not go on to attack
you. 5% of male flashers expose with an erect penis
and they can be dangerous. If you are unlucky
enough to be confronted by one of this tiny
minority, you should run or be prepared to defend
yourself. Women flashers are not thought to be
dangerous.

If you are a confident person, you'll probably
take seeing a flasher in your stride – perhaps even
find it mildly amusing. For other people it can be
traumatic. For some girls, for example, it may be
the first time that they have seen a male sex organ.
The shock and the unpleasant circumstances can
set up all sorts of negative associations for them
which they may take a long time to rid themselves
of.

You should report flashers to the police. Even if it
didn't disturb you, it may disturb someone else –
quite deeply too. In any case, you should tell your

parents/guardians or best friends about it. It's surprising how these occurrences can affect us without us realising it. Sharing the experience and talking it through helps to lessen its impact.

4. Touching and Rubbing

'I was sitting next to the window in the bus when the man next to me started rubbing his thigh up and down against mine and panting. I didn't know what to do. When my stop came I even said 'Excuse me' so I could get out. At least he looked embarrassed.'
Jenny (13)

'At the final it was like sardines on the terraces but I realised that the hand on my bum wasn't accidental. At half-time it eased up and I turned round to give him an earful, but I didn't know which geezer it was . . .'
John (14)

In crowded places like trains or shops or football matches, some people (usually men) like to rub their genitals against strangers. They are called 'frotteurs'. There are also people who like to take the opportunity to invade other people's private space by touching or brushing against their bums or breasts 'by accident'.

Sometimes boys who have been touched on the genitals find to their horror that they get an erection. This is a mechanical response to the

71

touching and it does not mean that you wanted to be touched by that person or that you led the toucher on.

If everyone is tightly packed, eg in a rush hour tube, it's sometimes hard to be sure whether you're being deliberately rubbed against or not. (I remember feeling very indignant and turning round to find someone's shopping bag jammed against my thigh.) If you are sure, try to move away or change seats. Say in a loud, indignant voice "Do you mind!"; "Keep your hands to yourself!"; "What's your hand doing there!" etc.

5. Peeping Toms

'My flat-mate's room was on the ground floor with a big bay window. The curtains didn't fit all that well and one night she saw a man looking in as she was undressing. He must have been crouching on the ledge. We all rushed out to chase him but he'd gone.'
Jane (17)

Peeping Toms are people (usually men, as the name suggests, but not always) who get sexual excitement by spying on unsuspecting people undressing, naked or having sex. They are also known as voyeurs.

Voyeurs tend to hang around swimming pools, changing rooms in shops, well known 'courting' spots etc, as well as peering through windows and keyholes. They are not thought to be dangerous
72

but it's obviously frightening and unpleasant to be watched in this way and know that you are featuring in someone's sexual fantasies.

Make sure that you can't be seen in your more private and intimate moments. Drawing the curtains when you're undressing is pretty obvious – although you'd be surprised how unaware some people are about being overlooked. Remember that when you switch on the light at night, your window is lit up like a film set from the outside. Some paper or bamboo blinds are opaque only in daylight. You should check that yours can't be seen through at night when the light's on.

If you live with your parents/guardians, finding a private place to spend time with your girl/boyfriend can be difficult. It's safer if you are able to spend time with her/him in your own home, but obviously this will depend on how relaxed your parents/guardians are, how trustworthy your girl/boyfriend is and how big your house/flat is. (In any case it's important that you have your own social space at home where you can invite your friends, if that's at all possible. Try and talk to your parents/guardians about it.)

If you do have to park in secluded places or wander down dark alleys take great care. Make sure there is no one around who is taking too much interest in you.

6. Whistling, Leering and Commenting

'I'm not the macho-looking type but I do hate

73

it when other boys call out things like 'Who's a pretty boy then!'. Sometimes they walk behind me and make sucking noises. It's frightening.'
David (16)

'The house across the road is being done up. When I leave for school in the morning the workmen call out "Hello darling!" and things like that. I don't mind; I think it's friendly and it makes me feel good.'
Pratibha (15)

When someone attractive walks down the street, some people indicate how they feel – by whistling or leering or shouting a comment. Of course, it's usually boys and men who do the whistling/leering and girls and women who are on the receiving end.

Some girls and women hate it – it makes them feel like an object rather than a person, a set of sexual parts for men to comment on. Other girls and women like it – it makes them feel sexy and attractive. Many girls and women feel in two minds about it – sometimes they feel angry and humiliated and sometimes pleased, depending on who pays them attention and in what way.

If you don't like this sort of attention there's not much you can do apart from ignoring it. You can also try indicating by your body language and by avoiding eye-contact that the attention is not welcome.

No girls and women enjoy crude comments

74

about bodies and sex ('Wouldn't mind giving you one, darling!') which reduce them to sexual objects, and it's quite unacceptable that they should have to put up with it. Girls and women are constantly confronted, in our society, with images of themselves in submissive, half-naked or naked poses promoting products or displayed in newspapers and magazines for male consumption. When you add to this the fact that the vast majority of sexual attacks are by males on females, it's hardly surprising that girls and women feel vulnerable to sexual comments and suggestions in a way that boys and men (whose bodies are not constantly exposed and under threat) find hard to understand.

A lot of leering and commenting has little to do with sexual attraction though. You'll have noticed that boys and men often do it to reinforce their status within their own group or gang and underline how macho they are. That's why they like to comment on other boys and men they think aren't 'masculine' enough. Sexual comments are also used against women who are in positions of power (eg female teachers) to try and belittle them. It's a male way of trying to define women as objects rather than as people and of keeping them in their place.

In an ideal world, perhaps we would all be freer, girls and women as well as boys and men, to express our admiration and pleasure in other people's attractiveness in a spontaneous way that would not harass or frighten them. As things are at the moment, boys in particular should realise how offensive and frightening many girls and women find their whistles, leers and comments.

7. Sexual Harassment and Assault at School

'We don't have machines for STs and tampons in the girls' toilets any more so if you come on at school you have to go to the office and ask. Sometimes there are boys in there and they can hear . . .'
Gloria (14)

'Our changing room has these big windows and the girls jump up and down outside and look in.'
Ravi (13)

'I had bad period pains and felt quite faint. I had to ask Mr McIlroy, my head of year, if I could go home. He said he was wise to girls trying to skive off and if I went home I couldn't come back in the evening for the school disco.'
Helen (16)

There are many different kinds of sexual harassment in schools. Sometimes it results from poor or unimaginative organisation within the school; students' privacy is not respected or they are put in embarrassing situations.

Sometimes people have funny ideas about what is 'normal' – how hairy boys' chests should be, how large girls' breasts should be, etc. In fact teenagers come in a lot of different shapes and sizes and they develop at different rates. Some look adult when they're thirteen, some don't develop until much later. Remember too that when you and your friends are fully developed adults, you will all be different. There is no one 'correct' size or shape for breasts, genitals or body hair.

School students and teachers often make life miserable by commenting unfavourably or cruelly on someone's appearance or by drawing attention to bodily changes that someone might feel self-conscious about.

> *'There was this man teacher who used to go up to the girls whose breasts were growing and say "You should be wearing a bra".'*
> Davina (17)

> *'When the boys were changing they noticed Stephen didn't have any pubic hair. They started shouting that he was a baldy. He wouldn't talk to anyone for ages after that.'*
> Andrew (15)

> *'They went through my schoolbag at break and hung my tampons all round the classroom.'*
> Lucy (14)

> *'At choir practice Mr Pembroke says "I want*

77

all of you to stick your chests out as you sing –
except those girls whose chests stick out
already." Bloody creep!'
Emily (16)

'When I'm embarrassed I get an erection
without meaning to. I have to put my hands in
my pockets so no one will notice. Once it
happened in swimming and everyone saw.
They keep calling me "the dirty pervert".'
Kieran (14)

If your school has a school council or parent-school association you could try to raise issues of sexual harassment such as these at their meetings. You may find some sympathetic teachers – these days teachers are increasingly aware of the need to stamp out sexual harassment as part of their professional responsibility to promote equal opportunities in schools.

Some problems (like changing rooms that can be overlooked) could be easily solved – they are just organisational problems. Obviously it's much more difficult to change people's attitudes and ways of behaving, especially if some teachers themselves harass students. These teachers usually do it because they think they are being trendy and want to ingratiate themselves with students. It's worth telling them straight that you don't like it and will complain if they don't stop. Do it as a group if you can. Unfortunately most schools have their crawlers who laugh uproariously at teachers'
78

jokes, no matter how sexist or sexual. You may not always get the support you need from your classmates.

> *'From time to time the boys will "get" a girl –
> a gang of about twenty will grab you and feel
> you up, put their hands up your shirt and
> everything. Once they did it to me in the
> corridor and there was old Mr Elm standing
> there. He didn't do nothing to stop them.'*
> Stephanie (16)

> *'There's this boy who thinks he's marvellous.
> If you meet him on the stairs he'll put his
> hands out like he's going to touch you down
> there. I tell him to piss off and he says "I could
> if I wanted to, you know".'*
> Dawn (15)

Sexual harassment at school can take very serious forms – boys who 'accidentally' touch girls' breasts or bums in crowded corridors or a group of boys who seize and assault a girl. If this has happened or happens to you, you should tell your parents/guardians and a teacher you can trust to take it seriously. It's important that people like that don't get away with it and don't do it again.

Double Standards

> *'Ricky went to Spain for his holidays and
> when he got back he told everyone he'd
> screwed this girl – he'd just had to lie there*

79

and she'd done everything. We all thought,
"Oh Yeah . . .".'
Paul (16)

The most insidious form of sexual harassment in school is the double standard that some girls and boys still have in their attitudes to each other. As teenagers become interested in sex and start dating, this double standard comes into force. Girls are classified as either 'slags' or 'tight bitches' – a no-win situation if ever there was one. If a girl is known to have slept with one boy, she's often considered fair game by all the other boys. Boys are expected to 'score' and have to pretend to be sexually active even if they're not and don't want to be.

And there's no recognition within this scenario that there can be other sexual preferences – only the most confident gay and lesbian teenagers will dare to 'come out' to their friends:

> *'I discovered I was gay at the age of twelve. I*
> *spent two years in utter confusion and then*
> *'came out' just before leaving school. It was a*
> *nightmare. I was called every name under the*
> *sun and used to get drunk every night to*
> *offset the pain.'*
> Jimmy (now 25)

It's not surprising that narrow and distorted views of sexual behaviour are still around. Sex has always been presented to boys as a 'fun' thing –

something non-threatening that they can control, while for girls sex has always been associated with the possibilities of violence, repercussions and responsibilities. As society changes, these polarised attitudes to sex are changing too and hopefully the double standard will one day be a thing of the past.

There is some evidence that today's teenagers are beginning to reject stereotyped sex-role expectations. Many still feel deep down, however, that boys 'naturally' get carried away by their sexual needs and can't help themselves, while girls 'naturally' take on the responsibility for letting or not letting sexual activity take place. These views are insulting to both boys and girls – boys are not just animals who can't help themselves, and girls are quite capable of being carried away by sexual passion. Decisions about sex should be a shared responsibility.

8. Rape and Sexual Assault

'I went for a walk early one morning, about 7am. He pulled me into a shop doorway and got me on the ground. He kept kicking me, especially on my head. As well as being raped my nose was broken and I had a fractured skull. I've got dyed blonde hair and my mum's divorced. I felt the police thought I was the type. They never caught him.'
Jane (17)

*'He suggested I got the early train so I could
have tea in his room before getting ready for
the May Ball. Only it wasn't tea he was
interested in. He made it quite plain that as
he'd spent such a lot on the tickets he was
going to get his money's worth. I kept trying
to push him off but he was so heavy and much
stronger than me. Afterwards he seemed
surprised how much I minded.'*
Claudine (17)

Rape is forcing someone to have sexual intercourse
against her/his will. In law this means that the rapist
penetrates his victim (into the vagina or the anus)
with his penis. Rapists are therefore always male as
the definition of rape is penetration by the penis.

But there are other kinds of sexual assault, many
quite as horrific as rape, which do not involve
penile penetration. Women and girls do carry out
such sexual assaults but relatively rarely. The vast
majority of sexual assaults are carried out by men
and older boys on women and girls and
(sometimes) on other men and boys. The victims
can be people of all ages from babies to women in
their nineties. Ugly people, good-looking people,
virgins and sexually active people have all been
the victims of rape or sexual assault.

Rape and sexual assault can include the forcing
of objects (bottles, sticks) into the vagina or anus,
peeing on the victim, forcing them to perform oral
sex, threatening and beating them.

No one ever enjoys being raped. Films and

books in which rape victims are shown enjoying being raped are telling lies about what rape is like.

Some people worry that because they have sexual fantasies about rape, in some way they may therefore secretly want or deserve to be raped. This is not so. Fantasies about rape are common because lots of people feel guilty about their sexual feelings and like to imagine a situation in which moral responsibility is taken away from them. There is no connection between fantasy about rape and rape in real life. Remember that you control your fantasies – you can't control being raped.

In real life, rape and sexual assault are quite simply crimes. The strange and frightening thing about them is that they involve using the physical acts of sex by which we express our love, trust and passion for another person, to inflict pain, degradation and suffering. It doesn't take much imagination to realise how humiliating and terrifying it is to be forced to have sex against your will. Many victims of rape and sexual assault take a long time to recover from their ordeal and suffer from anxiety and depression. They need time to rebuild their trust in their fellow human beings.

Stranger Rape and Sexual Assault

When people think about rape and sexual assault they usually imagine rapists to be weird looking strangers who jump out at their victims from behind bushes. This does happen (and that's why it's important to develop your self-preservation skills)

83

but it's pretty rare. Most rape and sexual assault occurs between people who know each other.

Acquaintance Rape and Sexual Assault

The majority of rapes (60% of those reported) and sexual assaults are committed by someone known to the victim – that is by someone who is perfectly 'normal'. Rapists and sexual assailants can be charming, friendly, successful, well-respected and well-liked people – the last people in fact whom you would think of as capable of committing such acts.

People sometimes find it difficult to understand why victims of rape or sexual assault don't just fight back – cross their legs, punch the assailant, run away. This attitude supposes that victims know clearly that they are in a rape/sexual assault situation and that they are in a position to use physical force to defend themselves.

Unfortunately it's rarely so simple. The majority of rapes/sexual assaults are committed in places where you would expect to be safe (a friend's party, your boyfriend's car, your home) by someone you know and probably assume to be trustworthy. The force used may be brute physical force or a weapon but it may also be subtle pressure that deliberately confuses you and puts you in the wrong ('You agreed to come here, you must have known what we'd do . . .'; 'You're just a cock-teaser, but you'll not get away with it this time . . .'). If you're a polite, well-behaved person yourself, it's often hard for you to grasp that this person really is attacking you sexually and isn't going to stop.

Our society's notion that males-must-push-for-sex/females-must-resist-sex inevitably leads to situations full of misunderstandings, coercion and confusion. How can you be sure that you both have the same expectations and are playing by the same rules?

One common-sense way is to have relationships with girls/boys who are as powerful as you but not more powerful. By this I mean people who are about equal to you in terms of age, experience and money. Obviously no one will be precisely equal to you in these respects (and it might be boring if they were) but overall, there needs to be an equal balance of power.

A lot of acquaintance rape and sexual assault occurs because there isn't a balance of power. If you're sexually inexperienced but decide to go out with someone who is much older than you and has a reputation for scoring, there will be an obvious power imbalance. You'll be playing with fire unless you're sure that this person is decent and trustworthy.

This is not, of course, to say that if you make a mistake and go out with someone who turns out to be untrustworthy, you *deserve* to be raped or sexually assaulted. You may be responsible for being silly and naive, but responsibility for rape or assault is *always* the rapist's or assailant's.

If You are Raped or Sexually Assaulted

If you are raped or sexually assaulted, try to keep calm. Try to say, as clearly as you can, that you don't want sex. If you don't know your attacker, try to memorise things about him (appearance, voice, clothes).

It is not possible to advise people who are caught in this situation whether or not they should try to defend themselves physically. It's something that only they can judge. It's almost always a good idea to try and talk yourself out of the situation. Try appealing to the attacker's better nature; would he like his sister/mother treated like this? etc. Crying, screaming or wetting yourself are all good off-putting tactics. Pretending to be pregnant or to have a period, or VD may help.

Sometimes the kind of physical defence tactics described on page 29 will work; sometimes it may be too dangerous to try to defend yourself physically. It's not worth being seriously injured or killed if you sense that submitting to the attack will at least mean that you live to tell the tale. There is a small number of violent sexual attackers who become more violent if you try to resist physically. Nothing matters more than staying alive.

After the Rape or Sexual Assault

You need help. Ring your parents/guardians or your best friends and (if you are a girl) the Rape Crisis Centre (the number will be in the phone book, or get it from directory enquiries). If you can't get hold of anyone or if you prefer, ring the police.

You may want to take a little time to decide whether or not to report the rape/sexual attack to the police. The Rape Crisis Centre worker and your family/friends will help you decide and go with you to the station. You may also need hospital treatment.

One of your first reactions will probably be to want to wash away all traces of your attacker – but by doing this you will be destroying vital evidence. Until you have had a chance to decide whether to report the rape/attack or not:

1 do not wash or bath
2 do not change or throw away the clothes you were wearing when attacked
3 do not drink alcohol or take drugs.

If you decide to report the attack to the police, you should do so as soon as you are able. Your appearance and behaviour following the attack will be used by them as part of the evidence that you were attacked.

Whether you decide to report the rape/sexual attack or not, you need the support of your family or friends and the Rape Crisis Centre while you recover. Even if you have not been physically injured, you will need to be tested for possible venereal disease or pregnancy.

Rape Crisis Centres are only available to girls and women. If you are a gay man, Gay Switchboard or Friend will counsel and support you; if you are heterosexual you will have to rely on family, friends and your doctor for support.

Should You Report Rape or Sexual Assault?

Unless you really cannot bear it, you should report rape and sexual attack to the police. Remember that your attacker may go on to attack others; you may be able to provide vital evidence that will lead to an arrest. The chief reason for reporting rape/sexual attack, though, is for your own satisfaction – this person should not be allowed to get away with it and you need to do whatever you can to see that he is caught.

These days the police are more sympathetic in their treatment of the victims of rape and sexual assault and will, in some forces, be able to call upon an officer with specialist knowledge and experience to deal with you. But you may be unlucky. There are still officers who think that some women and girls 'ask' for rape. You may be asked why you were out so late, why your skirt is so short etc, as though you were a criminal rather than a victim. That's one of the reasons why you need supportive people (family/friends/Rape Crisis Centre worker) with you.

You will be examined by a police doctor (you can ask for a woman doctor if you want to) who will take samples (eg of semen if there is any) that may help to identify the attacker. You will be asked to describe the rape/sexual attack. There is no need to worry about giving all the details – doctors and

88

police officers interview many victims of rape and sexual asault and know that such contacts sometimes involve different forms of sexual contact (eg forced oral sex, buggery) besides vaginal penetration. It doesn't matter if you don't know the 'correct' words for these things; just tell it as best you can.

Recovery From Rape or Sexual Assault

Recovery from rape or sexual assault is a gradual process. You need to get your confidence back and re-establish your normal life. To do this you need support from your parents/guardians and friends. You may also need counselling from someone experienced in helping victims of rape and sexual assault. Being attacked in this way is a heavy burden to carry and you need to talk the experience through with someone who can help you come to terms with it. Your doctor or Rape Crisis Centre worker will be able to tell you about counselling services in your area.

You may find that your family and community are not as understanding and helpful as you would like them to be. Your parents/guardians may be blaming themselves for the fact that you were attacked and be full of anger and guilt that it should have happened. They may even feel that they have failed you as parents/guardians.

There may be people in your community who are victim-blamers and who assume that *you* must somehow be to blame for the attack. It's an odd thing that people whose houses are burgled are not blamed for owning a video or antique silver and people who are mugged are not blamed for carrying money or jewellery, yet people who are raped or sexually assaulted are sometimes thought to be responsible for being attacked. Talk all this through with your counsellor or Rape Crisis Centre worker.

You may feel embarrassed at telling your parents/guardians how insecure you feel, especially in the first months after the attack. It's a good idea though, to be very practical about it – put extra locks on the doors and windows, establish a system of checks so that you feel absolutely safe. You need time to get your confidence back.

9. Incest and Abuse of Care

'It started when we were very small, four or five. First it was my sister but then he started on me as well. Usually when he was drunk. Mum was scared of him; she made out she didn't know. Funnily enough, when he died a couple of years ago, I felt sorry.'
Kevin (now 28)

'Grandad was always cuddling me and I liked that. I used to go down the allotment where he had this little shed. He said I was his special girl. Then when I was twelve he started touching me inside my clothes and making me do things to him. It hurt but I was too scared to say. He wasn't my grandad any

more; he was old and smelly and it hurt.'
Mary (now 20)

*'This violin teacher Mr Snow lived our way
and he started giving me a lift after orchestra.
He stopped the van one time and started
saying things and kissing me and everything.
He was about forty and had these nasty
sideburns. I wouldn't have a lift after that.'*
Sharon (13)

In Britain you are not allowed by law to marry or
have a sexual relationship with your father, mother,
step-father, step-mother, brother, sister, grandfather, grandmother, uncle or aunt. You can marry
or have a sexual relationship with your cousin
(including first cousins).

In some few families, sexual relationships
between 'forbidden' family members take place.
This is called incest. The most common form of
incest is a sexual relationship between a father and
a daughter, but it can also be between a father and
son, a brother and sister, a grandfather and
granddaughter, etc. Sometimes a child or
teenager will be sexually abused by more than one
family member – by their father and uncles, for
example.

Incest happens in all kinds of families – rich and
poor, white and black, middle, working and upper
class.

Some adults are in the position of being parents
although they are not biological parents (eg your

dad's live-in girlfriend, a lodger, your foster-father, your teacher, the staff of your children's home) and they therefore have the kind of responsibilities that parents have towards the children and young people in their care. It is illegal for them to abuse that care and form a sexual relationship with you.

Incest and abuse of care may involve actual sexual intercourse (penetration by the penis) or other kinds of sexual contact from touching of the genitals and breasts to oral sex. Sometimes this sexual abuse has been going on for years, since early childhood; sometimes it starts when a child reaches puberty. Sometimes only one child in a family is abused; sometimes all the children are victims.

Incest and abuse of care are crimes against the child or young person. The person responsible for these crimes is *always* the adult or older person who ought to know better. Incest and abuse of care are extreme examples of power imbalance in a sexual relationship – adults and the children in their care cannot by definition have a relationship in which both are equal partners.

The sexual acts involved in incest and abuse of care can be quite terryifying to the child or young person involved, but they can also be pleasureable. Sometimes victims of abuse feel guilty about what has happened because they enjoyed some of it or took part actively.

What you must remember is that our bodies are to some extent machines – press the right buttons and we experience sensations or reflex actions. The stimulation of certain parts of our bodies, particularly the genitals,can result in pleasurable feelings, perhaps orgasm. None of this means that you are in any way responsible for the incest or abuse of care, or that you 'really' wanted it to happen.

Telling About Incest and Abuse of Care

Those who have suffered incest and abuse of care report how difficult it is to tell anyone about what is going on. There is the fear of not being believed, the fear of splitting up the family or hurting some of its members (perhaps your mum doesn't know what's going on) and the fear that the abuser may take revenge on you.

It's vital though that you tell. Victims of incest and abuse of care not only have their childhood and youth taken away from them but they can suffer long-term effects which may affect their relationships later on in adult life. Sometimes victims keep quiet hoping to protect their younger brothers and sisters, only to find later that they too were being sexually abused and also did not tell.

> 'We had to write an essay at school on "An Odd Family" so I wrote mine on "The Odd Lodger" and told in detail what he was doing to me every day when I got back from school. When the teacher gave it back all she said was "There's no marks for filth in this school". That was that; she didn't understand what I was trying to tell her.'
> Patsy (now 25)

93

There have been cases of incest and abuse of care victims telling an adult what is happening only to find that they are not believed. These days, though, people are more aware that these things happen and more likely to believe you and respond sympathetically. This is because the problem has been brought to public attention by former victims of incest and abuse themselves. Some of these incest 'survivors' have formed an advice and help service for others who have suffered or who are suffering in this way.

Try telling a sympathetic adult you trust – a teacher, doctor, a relative in whom you have confidence, about what is happening to you. If you are not believed, go on trying to find someone you can rely on. You could phone the social services (in the phone book) and ask to speak to the duty social worker, or you could phone any of the agencies listed on page 102 of this book. They will believe you and will offer help and support.

You will probably find it hard to tell exactly what's been happening to you, especially if you've been bottling it up inside you for months or years. There's no need to worry though – police officers, doctors and social workers often deal with cases of incest or abuse of care and they know the kinds of things that you've been going through.

You may find that you have to repeat your story to several people – to the doctor, the police etc. This is often unavoidable but it can be a bit much. In some places video is now used used to record an incest/abuse of care victim's story so they don't have to keep repeating it. Videos will probably be allowed in court soon as well so that victims don't have to give evidence in person. By and large once you have managed to tell, you will find sympathetic and caring adults to help and support you.

VI **Finally**

This book has been about the dangerous, frightening and unpleasant ways that some people in our society express their sexuality and their idea of being a sexual person. Some of the things that I have discussed – incest, abuse of care, rape, for example – are illegal and our society punishes those who are convicted of having carried out such acts. Punishment is society's way of recognising that such acts are crimes and expressing its disapproval.

It would be a mistake, though, to think of sexual violence and abuse as something carried out by a few people who are sick in the head. Sometimes that's the case, but, as we have seen in the discussion on rape, there is often no obvious difference between sexual behaviour that leads to consenting sex between two people and sexual behaviour that leads to coercion and rape.

Our sexual behaviour is profoundly affected by the kind of society we live in and particularly in the way that girls are brought up to be female and boys are are brought up to be male. In general, boys still get the message that men should be sexually aggressive, powerful and in control while girls still get the message that women should be passive and sexually restrained. Standards of behaviour for the sexes are also still unequal. Even now it's not uncommon for a boy to assume that a girl who agrees to come up to his flat for coffee is actually agreeing to sex.

All this would be deeply depressing and appear to suggest that sexual violence is inevitable. There is some evidence from other societies, societies that value female attributes and promote sex equality, that sexual violence is much rarer than in our society. In the last years many people in our own society have rejected stereotyped expectations of women and men and have tried to establish a different way of relating to each other – a way which values sexual relationships and values sexual passion without linking it to violence and domination.

VII **Where to Get Help and Advice**

When you need help try to talk to someone you trust – perhaps your parents/guardians, your teacher or your doctor. If you don't have anyone you can talk to, contact the organisations listed here. Many of them are in London but some have branches in different parts of the country that they can put you in touch with. Most will deal with callers from outside London. London numbers start with 01. If you are in London do not dial the 01, just the rest of the number.

There is a national help and advice service for children and young people called Childline:
>   Childline
>   Freepost 1111 (no stamp needed)
>   London EC4 4BB
>   phone number 0800 1111 (the number is the
>   same wherever you live; the service is free
>   and open 24 hrs)

The Childline phone service is so busy that it's often difficult to get through. For some problems Childline cannot help you directly but will refer you to some of the other specialist organisations listed here.

Abortion – see **Contraception**

Abuse of Care – see **Incest**

Alcoholism – see **Drugs/Alcohol**

Contraception
For advice on contraception, abortion or
pregnancy counselling contact:
> British Pregnancy Advisory Service (BPAS)
> 7 Belgrave Road
> London SW1V 1QB
> (01) 222 0985

> Brook Advisory Centres
> 153a East Street
> London SE17 2SD
> (01) 708 1234

> Family Planning Association
> 27 Mortimer Street
> London W1N 7RJ
> (01) 636 7866

Counselling
The following organisations offer sympathetic and
impartial counselling on family and other
problems:

> Family Network Services
> National Children's Home (NCH)
> Stephenson Hall
> 85c Highbury Park
> London N5 1UD

Regional telephone numbers for this organisation:
Birmingham (021) 440 5970
Cardiff (0222) 29461
Glasgow (041) 2216722
Glenrothes (0592) 759651
Gloucester (0452) 24019
Leeds (0532) 456456
London (01) 514 1177
Luton (052) 422751
Maidstone (0622) 56677
Manchester (061) 2369873
Norwich (0603) 660679
Preston (0772) 24006
Swansea (0792) 292798
Taunton (0823) 73191

National Association of Young People's Counselling and Advisory Services (NAYPCAS)
17–23 Albion Street
Leicester LE1 6GD
(0533) 554775

Teenage Information Network (TIN)
102 Harper Road
London SE1 6AQ
(01) 403 2444 (London only)

Depression and Despair

Contact the organisations listed in COUNSELLING. If things are really bad ring the Samaritans. You will find the local number in the phone book or you can ask the operator to put you through directly. This is a 24hr service.

Drugs/Alcohol

For help with a drugs problem contact:

> Standing Conference on Drug Abuse
> (SCODA)
> Kingsbury House
> 1–4 Hatton Place
> Hatton Garden
> London EC1N 8ND
> (01) 430 2341

> Community Drug Project
> 30 Manor Place
> London SE17 3BB
> (01) 703 0559 (London only)

> Families Anonymous
> 88 Caledonian Road
> London N1 9ND
> (01) 278 8805 (London only)

For help with an alcohol problem contact:

> Al-anon (Groups in the UK and Eire)
> 61 Great Dover Street
> London SE1 4YF
> (01) 403 0888

> Alcohol Counselling Service (ACS)
> 34 Electric Lane
> London SW9 8JJ
> (01) 737 3579/3570

Incest/Abuse of Care

The following organisations will be able to contact someone in your area who will help you to deal with the situation and find you a place of safety:

The National Society for the Prevention of Cruelty to Children (NSPCC)
(branches in England, Wales and Northern Ireland)
67 Saffron Hill
London EC1N 8RS
(01) 242 1626

Royal Scottish Society for the Prevention of Cruelty to Children
Melville House
41 Polworth Terrace
Edinburgh EH11 1NU
(031) 337 8539/8530

The Church of England Children's Society
Edward Rudolf House
Margery Street
London WC1X 0JL
(01) 837 4299
(You don't have to be Church of England to contact this organisation)

Touchline (for people in the Yorkshire area)
(0532) 457777

Incest Crisis Line
32 Newbury Close
Northolt
Middlesex UB5 4JF

This service is run by incest survivors:
Richard (01) 422 5100
Shirley (01) 890 4732
Anne (01) 302 0570
Petra (Southend-on-Sea) (0702) 584 702
Chris (Carlisle) (0965) 31432

Incest Survivors Campaign
London: (01) 852 7432
        (01) 737 1354
Manchester (061) 236 1712
Dundee (0382) 21545
Belfast (0232) 249 696

Avon Sexual Abuse Centre (for people in the
Avon area)
39 Jamaica Street
Stokes Croft
Bristol BS2 8JP
(0272) 428331

Black Women's Campaign Against Child
Sexual Abuse
Black Women's Centre
(01) 274 9220

Taboo (for people in the Manchester area)
PO Box 38
Manchester M60 1HG
(061) 236 1323

Choices (for people in the Cambridge area)
(0223) 314438

International Organisations
Australia

Canberra
Children's Services – (062) 462625 (9am to 5pm)
Sydney
Child Protection and Family Crisis – (02) 818 5555 (24 hours)
2UE Kids Careline – (02) 929 7799 (9am to 5pm, Mon–Fri)
Darwin
Department for Community Development – (089) 814 733
Brisbane
Crisis Care – (07) 224 6855 (24 hours)
Adelaide
Crisis Care – (08) 272 1222 (24 hours)
Hobart
Department for Community Welfare, Crisis Intervention (002) 302 529 (24 hours)
Melbourne
Protective Services for Children – (03) 309 5700 (9am to 5pm)
Perth
Crisis Care – (09) 321 4144 (24 hours) or (008) 199 008 (toll free)

You can also contact through your local directory:

> The Police
> Lifeline
> Rape Crisis Centres

New Zealand
>
> *Auckland*
> Help – 399 185 (24 hours)

Canada
>
> The emergency number in Canada is 911.
> For help and/or advice:
> • Look in the telephone directory on the first
> page under Child Abuse
> • Ring the police or social services
> or
> • Contact: National Clearinghouse on Family
> Violence
> Health & Welfare Canada
> Ottawa
> Ontario K1A 1B5
> (613) 9572938
> who will refer you to someone in your area.

Keeping Safe/Self-Defence

Your local library should be able to advise you
on whether self-defence classes are available in
your area. They may be run as adult education
classes or by youth clubs, women's groups,
residents' associations or police volunteers.
>
> The Self Defence Project (London only)
> Women's Education Resource Centre
> Princeton Street
> London WC1R 4BH
> (01) 242 6807/2
>
> The Metropolitan Special Constabulary
> (London only)

New Scotland Yard
London SW1H 0BG

The Suzy Lamplugh Trust
14 East Sheen Avenue
London SW14 8AS
(01) 876 1838
is preparing a video and information pack on safety awareness.

Legal Rights

The Children's Legal Centre
20 Compton Terrace
London N1 2UN
(01) 359 6251

National Council for Civil Liberties (NCCL)
21 Tabard Street
London SE1 4LA
(01) 403 3888

Prostitution

At the time of writing there is only one organisation which specialises in helping young people caught up in prostitution:

Streetwise
PO Box 185
London SW5 9JR
(01) 373 8860
but the organisations listed under **Counselling** will also offer help and advice.

Rape/Sexual Assault

For girls and women:

The Rape Crisis Centre
PO Box 69
London WC1X 9NJ
(01) 837 1600 (24 hrs)
The number of your nearest Rape Crisis
Centre should be in the phone book.

For gay men and boys there is no equivalent to
the Rape Crisis Centre but help and advice can
be obtained from:
Lesbian and Gay Switchboard
BM Switchboard
London WC1N 3XX
(01) 837 7324

National Friend
BM National Friend
London WC1N 3XX
(01) 359 7371

For heterosexual men and boys there is no
equivalent to the Rape Crisis Centre. Help and
advice can be obtained from the organisations
listed under **Counselling.**

If you want to contact the police ring 999 or your
local police station (number in the phone book).

For support and counselling in the long term:
The Victim Aid Scheme
(01) 729 1252
Michael Alderman
PO Box 598

56 Harley House
Marylebone Road
London NW1 5HW
(01) 486 7490/854 8884

Runaways

For help and advice contact the organisations
listed under **Counselling**. You can also contact:

The Central London Teenage Project
c/o The Church of England Children's
Society
Edward Rudolf House
Margery Street
London WC1X 0JL
(01) 837 4299
The Central London Teenage Project has a
'Safe House' for runaways and will pass on
messages without giving away the runaway's
whereabouts.

The Piccadilly Advice Centre (London only)
100 Shaftesbury Avenue
London W1
(01) 434 3773

Message Home
(01) 799 7662
This is a 24hr phone service which offers help
to runaways. They will pass on messages
without giving the runaway's whereabouts.

The Samaritans
See the phone book for the local number.
They will give help and advice and pass on

messages without giving away the runaway's whereabouts.

Self-Defence – see **Keeping Safe**

Sex Education Books
You may be able to borrow these books from a library if you don't want to buy them:
Make It Happy: What Sex is All About by Jane Cousins (Penguin)
Boy Girl Man Woman: A Guide to Sex for Young People by Bent Claësson (Penguin)
Our Bodies Ourselves by the Boston Women's Health Collective (Penguin) – 'by and for women'.
Women's Experience of Sex by Sheila Kitzinger (Penguin)
So You Think You're Attracted to the Same Sex by John Hart (Penguin) – a sympathetic discussion of gay and lesbian sex.

Sexual Assault – see **Rape**

Sexually-Transmitted Diseases
If you suspect that you have a sexually-transmitted disease it's important to get medical help as soon as possible. Ring your local hospital and ask for the 'Special Clinic'.
For information and advice on AIDS you can ask at the local Special Clinic or contact:
The Terence Higgins Trust
BM AIDS
London WC1N 3XX
(01) 833 2971

Teenage Novels

These may be available from your local library if you don't want to buy them:

My First Love and Other Disasters by Francine Pascal (Lions)

I Love You, Stupid by Harry Mazer (Pan Horizons)

It's My Life by Robert Leeson (Lions)

Hey, Dollface by Deborah Hautzig (Lions)

The Catcher in the Rye by J.D. Salinger (Penguin)

Who Lies Inside? by Timothy Ireland (GMP)

Forever by Judy Blume (Pan Horizons)

First Love by Norma Klein (Pan Horizons)

Ruby by Rosa Guy (Gollancz)

Reflections of a Rock Lobster: A story about growing up gay by Aaron Fricke (Alyson)

Push Me, Pull Me by Sandra Chick (Women's Press Live Wires)

Tendencies to Violence

If you are worried that you have a tendency to sexual violence you should try discussing the problem with your doctor who might refer you to:

The Portman Clinic
8 Fitzjohns Avenue
London NW3 5NA
(01) 794 8262

The Tavistock Clinic
120 Belsize Lane
London NW3 5BA
(01) 435 7111

VIII Index